SHARP
SHOOTERS

NH
NEW
HOLLAND

SHARP
SHOOTERS

DAVID BIGGS

First published in 2004 by New Holland Publishers Ltd
London • Cape Town • Sydney • Auckland
www.newhollandpublishers.com
Copyright © 2004 New Holland Publishers (UK) Ltd

86 Edgware Road
London
W2 2EA
United Kingdom

14 Aquatic Drive
Frenchs Forest
NSW 2086
Australia

80 McKenzie Street
Cape Town
8001
South Africa

218 Lake Road
Northcote
Auckland
New Zealand

Copyright © 2004 in text: David Biggs
Copyright © 2004 in photographs:
New Holland Image Library (NHIL/Danie Nel) with the
exception of individual photographers and/or their
agents as listed on page 192.

ISBN 1 84330 718 9

PUBLISHER: Mariëlle Renssen
PUBLISHING MANAGERS: Claudia Dos Santos, Simon Pooley
COMMISSIONING EDITOR: Alfred LeMaitre
EDITOR: Gill Gordon
DESIGNER: Christelle Marais
DESIGN ASSISTANT: Jeannette Streicher
PICTURE RESEARCHER: Karla Kik
PRODUCTION: Myrna Collins

Reproduction by Hirt & Carter Cape (Pty) Ltd
Printed and bound in Singapore

2 4 6 8 10 9 7 5 3 1

★ ★

CONTENTS

SHOOTING

FROM THE LIP

THE FASTEST FUN IN THE WEST

Shooters, or shots, as they're known in some countries, are usually grouped together with cocktails in books of drinks recipes. This would seem logical at first glance, because both consist of mixtures of alcoholic beverages. But that's where the similarity ends. They're actually very different creatures.

Cocktails are supposed to be an elegant lubricant to intelligent conversation. Shooters, on the other hand, are designed to get you tipsy as quickly as possible.

The shooter probably had its origins in the northern European and Baltic countries — Scandinavia, Russia, Poland and northern Germany — where they still have a tradition of knocking back a small glass of very potent spirit in a single gulp.

Some of these areas are poor and, over the years, peasant drinkers had to learn to distil their own spirits from whatever came to hand. Man is an ingenious animal and wherever there's a rotting potato or a sheaf of mouldy corn, somebody will sooner or later find a way to turn it into alcohol. Whether the drink is called vodka in Russia or Poland, schnapps

9

in Germany and the Netherlands, or Akvavit in Scandinavia, in all these countries – with their frozen winters – a gulp of alcohol helps to keep out the chill and get the circulation going.

Although the ceremonies may vary slightly and the words differ from language to language, it is basically a matter of filling a tiny glass, looking your drinking partner in the eye and saying the equivalent of 'Cheers!' before tossing back the drink and holding out the glass for a refill.

But modern drinkers are an enterprising lot, always on the lookout for something new and daring when it comes to making a party go with a swing.

Shooters originated with a French drink called Pousse Café (literally a 'coffee chaser'), which was traditionally served with coffee after a meal and consisted of colourful layers of liquor built up in a straight-sided glass.

To celebrate Bastille Day, for example, you might be served a red, white and blue Pousse Café made of Grenadine, Cointreau and blue Curaçao. The original Pousse Café was more an exhibition of the pourer's skill than a serious drink.

Today's shooter was probably introduced via Canada, perhaps by an enterprising French barman with an eye to the modern market and an understanding of the current fashion for all things bright and new. Gradually the shooter in all its forms has grown into a drinks category on its own.

Shooters have developed their own drinking traditions. Some may be gripped in the lips, with hands held behind the back, or set alight and sipped from under the flames using a straw, but most are knocked straight back in one gulp.

Shooters are characterized by their layers, with each contrasting colour carefully poured to keep it separate from those above and below. It takes a steady hand and a good deal of trial and error.

The good news, of course, is that you can drink your errors.

The bad news is that this does not contribute to a steady pouring hand for the next round!

And while shooters may taste good, their names are usually in anything but good taste. When it comes to inventing names for shooters, good taste often goes out of the window. Taking the nature of the drink into account, it's not surprising that most of them come with names that are less than polite.

Unlike a cocktail party, a shooter party is loud and raucous and, sooner or later, a bit rude. You won't find many members of

Above Knocking back a few swift drinks has traditionally been a way to warm up when the temperature drops. Perhaps that's why skiing holidays are so popular!

the elegant cocktail crowd willing to ask the barman for a Love Bite, a Bloody Good Shot, a Horny Bull, or a Splash of Passion, but names like these fall easily from the lips of the shooter set.

So this is probably not the kind of book to give to your dear old granny for her 90th birthday. Unless, of course, you have a very swinging granny . . .

STEADY
AS SHE GOES

There's no limit to the number of shooters you can make if you use your imagination and have a very steady pouring hand. Look up almost any drinks site on the Internet and you'll find recipes for literally thousands of shooters. The real fun lies in creating your own variations and giving them appropriate names.

Considering the rapid effect of a good shooter, it may be best to prepare for a shooter party by making a number of drinks beforehand and keeping them on a tray in the fridge until they're needed.

Shooters are usually served in small, straight-sided shot glasses and the liquor is poured carefully over the back of a teaspoon to allow it to run gently down the side of the glass and settle on top of the layer below without blurring the dividing line.

In order to make sure the layers of colour stay separate, it is important to pour liquors with a high specific gravity (SG) before those with lower SGs, otherwise everything turns into a dull, monochrome mass. Or should that be mess?

This is not as straightforward as it might sound, because drinks producers seldom, if ever, reveal the SG of their products on the label.

What's more, different brands of the same kind of drink can have different specific gravities. One valuable clue is the alcohol content of the drink, which is printed on the label, either as a percentage or as ABV (alcohol by volume).

Higher alcohol content means lighter gravity. So begin with ingredients with less alcohol and work up to the really potent ones.

Brandies, for example, range from around 36% alcohol in some French Cognacs and Armagnacs, to a robust 43% in brandies designed to be mixed with cola, soda water or ginger ale to make a tall summer drink.

The recipes in this book are all tried and tested but, even so, you may occasionally have to vary the order of the ingredients to get the perfect result.

Practice makes perfect. But remember that too much practice makes perfectly drunk!

Above *Alcohol percentage varies from drink to drink, but will always be shown on the label.*

Below *The specific gravities of different drinks will cause them to float or sink. Enjoy experimenting !*

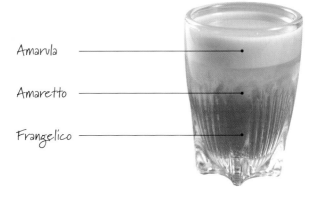

Amarula

Amaretto

Frangelico

Even though a shooter is in your mouth for just a second or two, there's no reason why it shouldn't taste great. You'll have the lingering aftertaste on your tongue for quite a while – at least until you reach for the next one.

Obviously you need a range of alcoholic drinks of varying colours to make shooters. Your drinks cabinet probably already contains the basics like vodka, tequila, rum and whiskey, but you'll need to brighten them up with a few strongly coloured liqueurs. Bright blue Curaçao, emerald Crème de Menthe, dark brown Kahlua and cherry-red Maraschino are just a few examples. Visit your local liquor store and select some attractive colours.

Interesting new liqueurs are regularly launched by liquor companies and some of these are

Above and left Sweet, sour, tart, tangy, spicy . . . these are some of the flavours you can use to create balance in your drinks. Don't be afraid to experiment.

definitely worth adding to your shooter repertoire, particularly if you like to experiment with new tastes and flavours.

Consider flavour balances when designing your own shooters. If you use a sweet liqueur, top it with a layer of something bitter or tart to create a balance. The Americano, for example, combines sweet white Vermouth with the bitterness of Campari, creating an ideal combination of tastes.

A cloyingly sweet liqueur can be made less sticky by adding a few drops of lemon juice or a dash of Angostura bitters.

Not all the ingredients in a shooter have to be alcoholic either. A layer of lime cordial gives a nice tart tang, while fruit juices add freshness and colour.

TOOLS

OF THE TRADE

As with any worthwhile hobby, shooter-making requires a few basic tools and supplies, and a willingness to spend time learning how to get it right. Part of the success of a good shooter lies in the ability to pour steadily and slowly, in order to keep the various ingredients separate.

For the basics, you'll need a set of small shot glasses, of course, plus a few thinnish teaspoons that fit comfortably into the mouth of the glass, and some pouring spouts.

Small teaspoons come in handy for gently layering the liquors. Hold the teaspoon curved side up, with the tip just touching the edge of the layer below. Trickle the liquor gently over the back of the teaspoon and onto the layer below. You may find it convenient to tilt the spoon slightly, even bend it, to suit your own style of pouring.

The easiest way to pour accurately is to buy a few spouts to fit into the bottlenecks, allowing the liquor to trickle out, rather than gush. These are available from all good bar equipment suppliers and consist of a tight-fitting cork or plastic stopper with a narrow pouring spout protruding from the centre. With practice you can control your pouring from a healthy glug to the merest trickle.

A medicine dropper is useful for adding small drops of colour to the surface of a creamy drink. It's fun, for example, to add a red heart to a Valentine Day shooter, a golden stripe to a Ginger Tom Cat, or a smiley face to a friendly shot. You can also use it to add a mysterious blob of colour to the middle of a drink.

Buy a sugar shaker if you often make shooters that require a sprinkling of cinnamon or cocoa powder, or use a purpose-made grinder of flavoured sugar or sweet spices. You'll need a small container of fresh cream for those sexily smooth shooters like the Angel's Tit or the Slippery Nipple.

If you make shooters on a regular basis, you may like to go technical and buy a hydrometer and tall glass cylinder for testing the specific gravity of each ingredient. This will tell you which one goes at the bottom and which go up in ascending order. It's not an essential item, but can add fun.

Other accessories, which you almost certainly already have in your kitchen, include a small bowl of water for rinsing spoons between pourings, a clean kitchen towel and a tray to stand it all on.

It might be a good idea to wear a barman's apron while you're experimenting. Things can get a little out of hand with shooters.

Opposite Grind spicy sugar over creamy drinks, or use a dropper to add decorative effects.

Below A pouring spout makes it easier to control the flow; a cocktail shaker is a useful addition; and shot glasses are essential.

ABSOLUT
Country of Sweden
VODKA
This superb vodka
was distilled

SHOOTER INGREDIENTS

The shooter's armoury should consist of as wide a range of colours and textures as possible. Obviously nobody without a professional bar can be expected to stock ALL the ingredients found in a modern shooter recipe book, but some are handy to have around anyway.

When planning a shooter party, start with the ingredients you have available, rather than beginning with a list of recipes. It would be daft to decide on a particular shooter if you have to scour the city for a bottle of one particular ingredient. Rather go with what is already in the bar cupboard.

You can build your drinks collection – and expand your range of shooters – gradually, by buying a single bottle of any interesting-looking drink from time to time. Go by colours at first. Start with a red drink, and add green, black, blue, and so on, as you progress.

Shooters require only a small dash of each ingredient, so the chances are your bottles will last a considerable time.

Here's a brief list of useful drinks to have on hand, with suggestions and hints for each.

AKVAVIT

A clear Danish spirit distilled from grain or potatoes and flavoured with caraway seeds. High alcohol. Popular in Nordic lands where it is drunk neat.

AMARETTO

A bittersweet almond-flavoured liqueur produced originally in Sicily. Great on its own over ice.

AMARULA CREAM

A South African cream liqueur flavoured with the berries of the marula tree, cream-coloured and nutty-flavoured.

ANGOSTURA BITTERS

Dark pink in colour and used a few drops at a time to add piquancy to a drink that might otherwise be considered too sweet.

BAILEY'S

The original, and still the best-known, Irish cream. There are plenty of wannabes.

BLACK SAMBUCA

A dark coloured Italian liqueur made from the witch elder bush and liquorice. The interesting liquorice flavour goes well with coffee. (See also Sambuca)

BLUE CURAÇAO

A colourful and tangy addition to any cocktail and a useful fresh acid flavour to cut through sweetness. (See also Curaçao).

BRANDY

Spirit distilled from grapes. Varies widely in strength. Colour ranges from quite dark amber to very pale gold. Adds a nice warming touch of flavour.

CAMPARI

An Italian bitters made from orange peel. Bright red in colour, with about 25% alcohol.

CHERRY LIQUEUR

A sweet concentrated cherry flavour and a useful pink colour.

COINTREAU

A very dry brandy-based liqueur made in France and Spain from oranges and orange peel. Clear, and highly alcoholic at about 40%. Useful if you want to set fire to your drink. A premium Triple Sec.

CREAM

Thick fresh cream adds a smooth velvety texture to many drinks. As it is light, it floats easily on top of most other ingredients.

CRÈME DE CACAO

Cocoa-flavoured liqueur made from cacao beans. It comes in two versions: clear (most often used in cocktails) and dark. Alcohol content of around 30%.

CRÈME DE CASSIS

A dark red, sweet, French liqueur made from blackcurrants. Has an alcohol content of about 20%. Often has a vintage date, as it tends to lose flavour with time. Great mixed with sparkling wine or white wine and soda.

CRÈME DE MENTHE

A fresh peppermint-flavoured liqueur, originally from France. Sometimes clear, but most often coloured deep green, which is probably best for the shooter creator. About 30% alcohol.

CURAÇAO

A traditional Caribbean liqueur made from bitter oranges. Comes in blue, green, orange and clear versions. Also made in Holland and Italy. High alcohol level (about 40%). A nice tangy addition to a drink. (Blue Curaçao turns orange juice green!)

FRANGELICO

An Italian liqueur made with toasted hazelnuts, vanilla berries and herbs. About 25% alcohol.

GALLIANO

A delightfully sweet Italian liqueur flavoured with herbs. A nice rich, clear, golden colour. Alcohol content about 35%.

GLAYVA

A Scottish liqueur based on whisky, flavoured with herbs and spices and having an alcohol content of around 40%.

GRAND MARNIER

An orange-flavoured liqueur from France. Made from Cognac, bitter Haitian oranges, spices and

vanilla. Alcohol at almost 40%. Colour varies, with darker amber versions higher in alcohol.

GREEN CHARTREUSE

A green, herb-flavoured liqueur produced in France and Spain. Originally made by Carthusian monks to treat cholera patients. Very high alcohol content. There is also a milder yellow version.

GRENADINE

A nonalcoholic red-coloured syrup made from pomegranates. Very useful for adding both colour and sweetness.

IRISH CREAM

A smooth cream liqueur traditionally made from Irish whiskey, cream, chocolate and neutral spirits. Some versions use

brandy instead of whiskey. Low alcohol (about 16%). A useful creamy off-white colour.

JÄGERMEISTER

A bitter, dark red liqueur from Germany. A complex blend of herbs and spices, it is said to have great digestive properties.

KAHLUA

A coffee-flavoured liqueur originally from Mexico. Alcoholic strength usually about 26%. Nice dark brown colour.

KIRSCH

A clear, cherry-flavoured German liqueur made from cherry pips, traditionally matured in earthenware casks. High alcohol content of 43%. Useful for the top layer of a shooter.

KIRSCHWASSER

A cherry brandy made in the Black Forest in Germany. Clear in colour. About 40% alcohol.

KIWI LIQUEUR

A New Zealand liqueur made from kiwi fruit. Pale green colour and about 40% alcohol.

KÜMMEL

A clear Dutch liquor distilled from grain and flavoured with caraway seeds. It's available in various alcohol strengths.

LIME CORDIAL

Nonalcoholic concentrated lime flavour with a deep golden-green colour. Useful to add a tangy bite to sweet drinks.

MARASCHINO

A clear, dry liqueur made in Italy from marasca cherries, with an alcohol content of about 30%.

MARASCHINO CHERRIES

Cherries steeped in Maraschino liqueur and dyed bright red or green. Useful as a garnish or decoration for cocktails.

MIDORI

A Japanese liqueur made from honeydew melon. Bright green in colour and with an alcohol content of about 30%.

OUZO

A clear aniseed-flavoured liqueur from Greece. Turns milky when mixed with water. Around 40% alcohol (sometimes lower).

PARFAIT AMOUR

A violet-coloured French liqueur, delicately flavoured with orange peels, enhanced by rose petals, vanilla and almonds, with a name that means 'perfect love'. The alcohol level is about 30%.

A version is made in the USA from lemons, citron, coriander and sugar, with a deeper purple colour. Also about 30% alcohol.

RUM

A strong West Indies spirit made from distilled molasses. Colour ranges from clear to dark brown, depending on the amount of caramel colouring used or the length of time in oak barrels. Alcohol strengths vary widely.

SAMBUCA

An Italian liqueur made from an infusion of witch elder and liquorice. Comes in black and white versions. A rather high alcohol content at 40%. Also known as Sambucco. (See also Black Sambuca)

SCHNAPPS

Generic name for a clear German spirit with a high alcohol content (about 45%) and plenty of kick. Flavoured with various fruits.

SOUTHERN COMFORT

An American drink made from bourbon whiskey flavoured with orange and peach. High alcohol content at about 50%.

TEQUILA

A powerful Mexican spirit distilled from the fermented juice of the Agave plant.

Most tequilas are unaged *blanco* (white or silver) or *joven* (gold) versions, but some are aged in wood for up to a year. A global favourite, best known in Margaritas. Alcohol around 40%.

TRIPLE SEC

A very sweet white Curaçao made from oranges.

VAN DER HUM

A sweet South African liqueur distilled from tangerines, brandy and various herbs and spices. Amber or clear in colour. About 30% alcohol.

VODKA

A clear, almost flavourless spirit distilled in Russia, Poland (or almost anywhere else). A sneaky way to add alcohol to a drink without altering the taste. Much favoured by lunchtime drinkers as it leaves no alcohol breath. Alcohol varies up to about 45%.

WHISKEY

The spelling used to denote that it is not Scotch whisky, which is spelled without the 'e'.

WHISKY

The golden Scottish liquor distilled from malted barley and pure water. Comes in many guises, including single malt, blended whisky and vatted malt. Usually about 40% alcohol.

Don't use single malt whisky in cocktails or shooters. Any Scot present will probably faint at the sacrilege (and the price should put you off anyway!). Rather use a cheaper blended whisky, or an American Bourbon whiskey (note different spelling).

SHOOTING GAMES

Drinking games can be a fun part of any shooters party. They add an element of competition and provide a legitimate excuse to down an extra drink or two. And the good thing with drinking games is that it is as much fun losing as winning.

A shooter party is not at all like an elegant cocktail party, which is supposed to be held together by erudite and witty conversation, with the drinks merely there to aid the process of social bonding.

Shooter parties are for fast fun, and the conversation is likely to become very rough after a short while, getting positively rude as the evening progresses.

Drinking games traditionally require little skill and no intelligent conversation. Almost any indoor game can be adapted as a drinking challenge, the loser having to down a shooter as a forfeit each time. Here are some examples to get the party going.

SHOOTERS CRAPS

The simplest drinking game

All you need is a pair of dice and a good capacity for alcohol.

Any number of people can play and each player starts with a shooter at his or her elbow.

Players roll the dice in turn and anybody who shoots a score lower than seven must down the shooter and be issued with a fresh one.

The winner is the last one still upright.

MATCHES

One of the oldest drinking games around

Any number can play, and each player is issued with three matches. At a signal, all the players place a closed fist on the table, each containing some matches – or none.

Each player in turn tries to guess the total number of matches on the table. It could range from zero (if all the hands are empty) to three times the total number of players (if everybody is holding three matches).

Each time a player guesses correctly, that player discards one match. The first player to lose all his matches is the winner and is rewarded by being allowed to down a shooter of his choice.

Alternatively, the last player to lose all his matches is the loser and has to down a drink of the winner's choice.

CARDINAL PUFF
A more complex game requiring deep concentration

This is more of a spectator sport than a mere game, and the cheers and boos of the spectators add to the hilarity.

The 'leader' in this game sits facing the challenger. Each of them holds a long drink (probably a beer) and there should be several shooters lined up between the two. The leader begins with a simple toast: 'Here's to Cardinal Puff for the first time'. He then raises his beer glass, drinks the toast and sets it down. The challenger must follow every move and word of the leader.

The second toast is more complicated and could be: 'Here's to Cardinal Puff-puff for the second time', followed by a thump on the table and a scratch of the ear, all of which must be copied.

Each time the challenger makes a mistake, he or she must down one of the lined-up shooters. As the toasts progress the leader can think up more complex bits to add; such as a double hand clap, or toasting Cardinal Puff-puff-poof.

The sneaky thing about this game is that, as the challenger downs more and more shooters, so his concentration disappears and he starts losing more rapidly. The challenger wins if he is still coherent by the time all the shooters have disappeared.

SHOOTER'S STRETCH
For the more physical members of the party

The trick here is to place a shooter on the floor about a metre in front of the competitor, who must keep feet and hands behind a line. He then has to stretch out, without touching the floor with his hands, take the shot glass in his mouth and down it, still without hands.

The next contestant must try to equal the distance achieved by the first, and if they both manage to swallow the shooter, the second round takes place with the glasses a little further away.

Obviously the winner is the drinker with the furthest reach. Other members of the group can then challenge his stretch in subsequent rounds.

Shooter's Stretch takes good balance. The more you win, the poorer your sense of balance is likely to be, so it's a game with a built-in handicap.

SHOOTER RECIPES

Americano

This is a shooter version of the **classic highball drink.** In the traditional way, it combines the **sweetness** of one ingredient (sweet Vermouth) with the **bitterness** of the other (Campari).

Start by swirling a dash of **Angostura bitters** around the shot glass to coat it. Now pour in half a glass of **sweet vermouth** and slide **Campari** on it to form the top layer. A few drops of **fresh lemon juice** could add a **zing** to this if you feel it needs it.

Angel's Kiss

Here's a **creamy dream** of a shooter. I'm told you'll know **exactly** how it got its name **after** tasting one.

Start with a layer of **crème de cacao** and carefully add consecutive layers of **sloe gin**, **brandy** and **fresh cream** floated on top.

Heavenly? Yes!

Angel's Tit

It doesn't take much **effort** to see how this
attractive little drink got its name.
It's also one of the few shooters
that is traditionally served with a **garnish**, so the
little red nipp ... er ... cherry
on top is quite **important**.

One part of **crème de cacao**,
one part **maraschino liqueur** trickled
on top, followed by a layer of **thick cream**.
Carefully top with a
maraschino cherry.

Army Green

Goodness knows how this little shooter got its name. It's **not** green and there's **nothing** particularly military about it. Just **mix** and **fire away.**

Start with **white rum**, add a layer of **black sambuca** and top with **triple sec**. Maybe the **stripe** in the middle reminded a barman of his favourite **lance corporal**.

Autumn Leaf

This is a good shooter for the **beginner**, because it **doesn't** really matter if the colours do **blend a little**. They'll end up looking like an **attractive** autumn leaf anyway.

Start with a layer of green
crème de menthe, slide a layer of
sweet Galliano on top, then add
a layer of **dark brandy**.
If they blend a little you'll have a gradation of colour
from green, through gold to autumn brown.
Finish it off with a sprinkling of **nutmeg**.

Bailey's Chocolate Cherry

Here's a **pretty** little layered shooter that's quite **easy** to build.

Begin with a layer of **red grenadine** syrup for sweetness and colour, slip on a **layer of Kahlua** and top with a rich layer of **Irish cream**. It **tastes** as **good** as it **looks**.

Banana Split Shooter

Remember those big sticky parfaits
you enjoyed as a child?
Here's one for the grown-ups.

Start with one layer of banana liqueur,
add a layer of vodka and top with a generous
layer of Irish cream.

Garnish with a juicy
maraschino cherry
for old time's sake.

Bastille Bomb

Your **French friends** will appreciate this **red, white and blue** drink if you serve it on Bastille Day, July 14. It was created to commemorate the **storming** of the Bastille in 1789.

Build it up with a layer of
red grenadine, a layer of **clear Cointreau** and one of **blue Curaçao.**
For a really dramatic finish, get the Cointreau on top
and light it before swallowing it down fast enough to
avoid lip burn or a moustache fire.
Voilà!

Bird Dropping

This **quaintly** named little beverage obviously gets its name from its looks, but rest assured, the **tastebuds** will take to the **wing** after this offering.

Start with a layer of **blackberry brandy or liqueur**, carefully float a layer of **tequila** on top and finish off with a layer of **cold milk**. Look familiar?

(Depending on brands, the blackberry liqueur and tequila might need to change places.)

Bloody Good Shot

This is the shooter version of the ever-popular Bloody Mary. Some drinkers say it's the very best way to enjoy vodka and tomato juice.

Fill one-third of a shot glass with lemon juice. Slide an equal layer of tomato juice onto this, trying to keep the two separate (if they mix it's not a tragedy). Next slip an equal layer of vodka onto the juice, and float a few drops of Worcestershire sauce on the top. Very refreshing!

Blue Balls

Not all shooters have to be poured carefully in layers of colour. Some can be **mixed** like an ordinary cocktail, to be **swallowed, shooter-style,** in a **single gulp**. This is one of them.

★ ★

Mix together equal quantities of
**blue Curaçao, Malibu,
peach schnapps** and **lemon juice**.
Shake with **ice cubes** and strain into shot
glasses. It makes a very good aperitif and
gets a party off to a **swinging start**.

Blue Bastard

This is one of those shooters that are usually **mixed** in some quantities before the party starts, so you can keep the **shots coming** as the guests **knock them back**. The secret is the blueberry schnapps, sometimes difficult to find.

Mix equal quantities of
blueberry schnapps,
clear sugar syrup, triple sec
and a splash of **vodka** to taste.
Shake over **ice** and serve in shot
glasses to be tossed back fast.

Blue Cobbler

Blue drinks always have a **shock appeal** because so few of the things we drink are naturally blue. This little shooter is based on the **classic** brandy cobbler, with the **difference** that blue Curaçao is used.

Start by trickling a little **Angostura bitters** in a shot glass and swirling it to coat the inside. Add a splash of **lemon juice** then float a layer of **brandy** on top of it. Finish with a carefully poured layer of **blue Curaçao.**

Blue Polar Bear

This is a truly **refreshing** summer shooter that can be **mixed** in some quantity and poured as required.

In a **shaker**, place **three ice cubes** and add generous helpings of **vodka** and **peppermint schnapps,** followed by a splash of **blue Curaçao. Shake** and serve in shot glasses.

Bob Marley

This drink is obviously based on the **traditional Rasta colours** and makes a very **pretty** shooter.

Start with a layer of **red grenadine syrup**, add a neat layer of **Advokaat egg cream** and finish with a layer of green **crème de menthe**.

Very pretty, mon.

Bogey

Too many of these could bring out the **evil** or mischievous **spirit** in you (well, where do you think the **bogeyman** gets his name from?)

This ethereal sprite consists of neat layers of tropical **coconut** liqueur, green **Midori melon** liqueur and yellow **crème de banana,** with a couple of blobs of **Irish cream** dribbled on top. It certainly **tastes better** than its name.

Brain Haemorrhage

Well . . . the name alone should act as a **warning**!

Fill a glass to two-thirds with **peach schnapps**, then add a layer of **Irish cream.** Finish with a few drops of **grenadine.**

Bush Pig

The top layer of this **fierce** little drink is traditionally **set alight** before shooting it back, **flames** and all. Maybe it would be more correct to call it the bush fire.

Start with a layer of **vodka,** then add a layer of **Amaretto** and finally a layer of **dark rum.**

Ignite and demolish.

Butterball

Here's a **really creamy drink** that isn't difficult to name.

Take one part of Irish cream,
one part of strong, cold coffee
and one part of
butterscotch schnapps.
Pour them carefully and separately into a
shot glass to create a swirled effect,
rather than making layers.
Different and delicious.

B52 Classic

This is one of every barman's standard classic shooters. Your first taste will show you why it's so popular.

Pour one-third of a shot glass of **Kahlua** and gently slip an equal amount of **Irish cream** on top of it.
Finally fill the glass carefully with a layer of **Grand Marnier.**
There. You've created a **classic.**

B52 – the Dangerous Way

Now here's a drink that's **not** for the **faint-hearted**. It's also a real **challenge** for the barman.

Start with a layer of **Kahlua** and float a layer of **Irish cream** on top of it, finally, add a layer of **Cointreau.**

Now comes the tricky part.

Light the **Cointreau,** grab a drinking **straw** and drink the shooter from the bottom before the straw catches alight.

Talk about going down in **flames!**

Cactus Flower

Here's a **prickly** little drink for the **brave**. It may be **advisable** to have a glass of **iced water** handy for afterwards.

Start by pouring a layer of **Tabasco sauce** into the bottom of a glass, and then carefully fill the glass with **tequila**, taking care not to allow the two to mix. The whole point is that the Tabasco should add a burst of fire **after** the tequila has provided the initial flames.
Talk about **fighting fire** with **fire**.

Candy Cane

This one's a **pleasantly cooling** summer shooter to test the barman's **skill** and **steadiness**.

Carefully layer **grenadine syrup**, **crème de menthe** and **peppermint schnapps** in a shot glass to create pretty stripes.

Tastes as **good** as it looks.

Chicken Dropping

In spite of its rather **unappetizing**
name, this pleasant little drink is
well worth trying.

Start by pouring a layer of very cold
(almost frozen) **orange juice.**
Slide a layer of **Jägermeister** onto it and
top with a carefully layered dollop of
peach schnapps.

Cluck it back. Er, sorry, chuck it back.

Crimson Hotpants

It's not difficult to guess **how** this little drink got its name. It's **quick** and **easy** to make and will certainly provide a **tingle**.
It also **slips** down nice and **slowly**.

Just mix equal parts of **Jägermeister** and **blackberry brandy**.

Pour into a shot glass and let its **silky** smoothness **seduce** you.

Dr Evil

This is a **nasty** looking shooter that **won** its name on **looks** alone.

Start with a layer of **brandy** or **Jägermeister**, slip on a layer of **gin** and top with a layer of **vodka**.

The top two could be mixed,

as they look the same, but try to keep them

apart for the taste explosion it will cause.

Shoot it **down.**

Electric Jelly

(or jello for Americans)

Here's a **novel idea** to end a meal and get the rest of the evening's **pleasures** swiftly under way. The day before your party, make up a packet of jelly powder of whatever flavour you choose. **Lemon** or **lime** are good ones.

Instead of the recommended quantity of water, use **half water** and **half vodka**, taking care not to boil it, or the alcohol will evaporate. Pour into shot glasses or tiny cups and leave overnight in the **refrigerator**. Remember vodka will require a slightly lower setting temperature than water. When set, the jellies can be served as **dessert,** with small teaspoons.

Fire Bomb

This is a **mixed** shooter, rather than a layered one, and it obviously gets its name from the **sting** of the Tabasco sauce. The other ingredients are **pretty hot** too, so **be warned!** You may like to have a chaser of iced water standing by to douse the **flames.**

One part **vodka**, one part **tequila**, one part **Jack Daniel's** and a generous dash of **Tabasco sauce.**

Light fuse. Stand clear.

Flaming Cow

This is quite a **soothing** little shooter,
as you get the **flames first** and **then** the
cold milk to **heal** the throat.
It's a **simple** recipe too.

Place a layer of **cold milk** in a shot glass, then
slide on a generous layer of **Jack Daniel's.**

Quite a pick-me-up.

French Kiss

This **pretty** little layered drink is **fun** to make and **slides** as **happily** over the **lips** as its name implies.

Start with a layer of dark crème de cacao, then slide Irish cream onto it and finally, top up with almondy Amaretto.

Sexy? Oui?

Ginger Tom Cat

This is a drink for the barman with an **artistic eye** and a **steady** hand. Properly made, it really does take on the colours of a **tousled** ginger **kitten**.

★

Start with a layer of **ginger ale,** carefully add a layer of **peach schnapps** and finally, float small drops of **Irish cream** over the surface of the drink to create the right tabby pattern. For a variation, try for **stripes** of Irish cream and call it a **tiger.**

Glayva Sour

This pretty and **refreshing** little shooter depends on the **Scotch** whisky-based liqueur for its **unique** character.

Start with a layer of **fresh lemon juice,**
slip a generous layer of **Glayva** onto it
and top it with a spoon of
freshly whipped **egg white.**
It's said to keep out the Highland chills and
ward off colds. Och aye!

Golden Nipple

It's amazing how many **creamy** shooters are named after **somebody's** nipple. Maybe lonely barmen just like to **dream**.

Start with a layer of Goldschläger, add a careful layer of butterscotch schnapps and top with a sexy layer of Irish cream. Slip it down with closed eyes. See? A dream comes with every drink.

Gorilla Snot

This drink retains its **popularity** mainly because of the name. It's a nicely **macho thing** to be able to front up to the bar and say: 'Gimme a glass of gorilla snot'.

To make it, carefully layer **green Midori** melon liqueur, then **yellow crème de banana** and add a good dribble of **yellow Advokaat** on top.

It looks truly disgusting, but has rather a nice tropical flavour. Well, it would, I guess.

Great White Shark

This is probably **not** considered a true shooter by **perfectionists**, because the ingredients are **mixed** together, rather than being layered, but it's **fun**, nonetheless and a good **circulation booster** after a chilly ocean swim.

★ ★

Pour a generous helping of **tequila** and a couple of dashes of **Tabasco sauce** over **ice cubes,** shake and strain into a shot glass. Open the **jaws** and gulp it down.

Gigantickle

This is a **pleasant** drink that can be served as a mixed shooter, layered shooter or, with more orange *juice* in the mixture, as a longer *cocktail* drink.

⭐

Mix equal parts of **Southern Comfort, raspberry liqueur** and fresh **orange juice.**
Shake with **ice cubes** and pour into shot glasses to be swallowed in a single gulp.
For a layered shooter, begin with the o-j, then add raspberry liqueur, followed by Southern Comfort.
Does that **hit** the **spot**?

Gender Bender

Here's a wicked little shooter that's so **packed** with alcohol that you **probably** won't know whether you're Arthur or Martha afterwards, hence the name.

Carefully layer blue Curaçao, Jack Daniel's, dark rum and Irish cream. You may need to vary the order, depending on the brands involved, as alcohol content and specific gravity will differ from brand to brand. It will be fun getting them straight, anyway.

Hand Grenade

This fun drink is obviously named for the way in which it is drunk. Also, hand grenades were referred to as 'pineapples' in the Chicago gangster days. A great starter for a party!

You'll need a fresh pineapple, a generous dollop of vodka and an equal quantity of 7-Up or Lemon Twist drink.

Cut the pineapple into strips and soak them in the vodka and 7-Up mix in the fridge overnight.

To serve, stand a pineapple strip in a shot glass and top it up with the vodka mixture.

Ready to fire? Grip the pineapple 'pin' between the teeth, pull it out and chomp it down and follow it fast with the rest.

Harley Davidson

I think this pleasant little shooter got its name simply because its main ingredient originates in the land of the **legendary motorcycle.**
It's certainly quieter than its namesake, although too **many** of them could have you **roaring.**

Start with a layer of **black sambuca** and slide an equal layer of **Jack Daniel's** on top.
You'll enjoy the fragrant liquorice flavour.

Heaven and Hell

It's not hard to see how this **attractive drink** got its name.

Start by creating hell, using a layer of **black sambuca.** Then add a celestial layer of **clear Pernod.** Finally, create a few fluffy clouds by adding tiny **drops of water** to the Pernod. Halleluiah! This should raise your spirits.

Horny Bull

This is a good shooter for **beginners,**
as all the ingredients are **clear,** so
it doesn't really matter if they don't
stay **neatly** layered.

Start with a shot of **vodka,**
slip some **tequila** on top and finish
with a topping of **white rum.**

Add a touch of drama by mixing a few drops of
Angostura bitters with the tequila.

It adds colour, and a zingy flavour too.

Hot Damn!

The name was probably the first thing the customer said after **downing** one of these **robust** little drinks. It certainly packs a punch.

★

Start with a layer of **whiskey,** follow it with a layer of **orange juice,** then one of **white rum** and finally a layer of **vodka.**

It might work better with the **O-j** at the bottom, depending on the different brands of liquor.

Irish Monkey

This little dash of **jungle juice** is easy to make and rather delicious. If you're introducing it to a party of friends, have **several** standing by, **ready-made**, in the fridge.

Start with a layer of clear **banana liqueur** and slide a layer of **Irish cream** on top, keeping the layers cleanly separate.
If you're feeling very creative, a couple of tiny drops of **crème de menthe** on top adds a jungle look.

Italian Valium

I am **assured** by Italian friends that this is a very **calming** drink. Although often referred to as an 'IV' it should **not** be administered **intravenously!**

Just mix two parts of **Amaretto** with one part of **gin.** Stir well.

Serve in a shot glass, to be swallowed in one gulp.

Wait for the **calmness** to settle over you.

It may take a second dose.

Jamaica Dust

This shooter is a little **different**, as it is **mixed**, rather than layered. Try it, and enjoy a taste of **island style**.

Stir together equal parts of **white rum, pineapple juice** and **coconut liqueur.**

Pour into a shot glass and dust with a generous topping of **cinnamon.**

Jelly Fish

Here's a challenge for the
artistic shooter-pourer.

Begin by pouring a layer of
dark crème de cacao into the
glass and slip a shot of **Amaretto**
onto it, keeping the division clear.
Slide **Irish cream** onto that and decorate the
top with drops of **grenadine syrup.**

Tastes better than it looks.

Let's Tango

Get in step with a nice little touch of Latin America.

Start with a layer of **black sambuca**,
add a layer of **white rum**
and top with a layer of **triple sec**.
Start the music and slide it down,
but remember, it takes **two to tango**.

Love Bite

Here's a romantic — and very dramatic-looking — little splash of colour that's ideal for serving on Valentine's Day. Always make two. They don't taste anything as good served singly.

Start with a layer of **Parfait Amour** and float a layer of **cherry liqueur** on top of it. Add a final layer of thick, sweet **cream.**

Here's lookin' at you, kid.

Melon Ball

If you're looking for a shooter that won't embarrass your maiden **aunt** – either by its name or the fierce effect it has on her – here's a **pleasant fruity** drink to try. But don't blame us if it has your aunty **dancing** on the **table**.

Pour a layer of **vodka** into a shot glass, slide a layer of **Midori melon** liqueur onto it and top it with a layer of fresh **pineapple juice**.
It looks as **good** as it tastes.

Mudslide

No problems with this name.
It's suitable for **polite** company and it won't matter if it mixes and looks a bit **muddy**.
It'll still slide down just as easily.

Start with a layer of **Kahlua,**
slip a layer of **Irish cream** on top and finish with a thin layer of **vodka,**
trickled on really slowly to prevent mixing.
Here's **mud** in your **eye!**

Nasty Union Jack

This is a **colourful,** and rather **potent,** little drink. If you're looking for an **excuse** to drink it, they do say it helps to **cure colds.**

Place a layer of red Aftershock liqueur in the bottom of the glass, layer some blue Curaçao on top and finally add a layer of sambuca of any colour.

(White is patriotic, but black is more dramatic.)

Nutcracker

This shooter is no threat to your **manhood**, in spite of its slightly aggressive name. It's based on nut liqueurs and topped with Amarula Cream, which is made from the berry of the African **marula** tree. At a certain time of the year the berries **ferment** and the elephants and baboons that eat them get **rolling drunk**. Who says humans are the only animals who can enjoy a good binge?

Start with a layer of **Frangelico,** slide a layer of **Amaretto** on top and finish off with the layer of **Amarula Cream.**

When you've seen what this stuff does to an elephant, you'll approach this little drink with great **respect.**

Orgasm

Here's another drink that might take a little **bravado** to order. On the other hand, it's a handy **icebreaker** for a shy host.

'Would you like an orgasm?' is guaranteed to get conversation started. It's a **quickie** to make, too.

Start with half a glass of **tequila** and add an equal amount of **Irish cream.**

Whether it stays separate, or **merges** into a creamy blend, the result is orgasmic. Yes?

Original Sin

Go on, try it! Like so many of life's pleasures, this one is very tempting.

Start with a layer of emerald **crème de menthe** and slide a layer of **Irish cream** on top.

Don't forget to **share** it with your **friends.**

Pancake

This tasty little shooter uses **Cape Velvet**, a South African brandy-based cream liqueur. If you can't find this delicious drink, Irish cream makes a good **substitute**.

Pour half a shot glass of cinnamon-flavoured **Aftershock,** then float a layer of **Cape Velvet** on top.
Dust with cinnamon to enhance the effect.
The **seductive** blend of cream and spice will have you holding out your glass for a refill.

PS I Love You

Here's a **romantic** little drink to get the evening off to a **good** start.

Begin with a layer of Grand Marnier and slide on a layer of Irish cream. Trickle a little crème de menthe on top. (Try to make a heart shape. There's a challenge!) Dust with a little nutmeg for effect. Isn't love worth the extra effort?

Psychedelic Barney

Remember that **bouncy purple** dinosaur in the kiddies' TV programme? This is his **portrait** after a **bad trip**.

Start with a layer of **blue Curaçao**, slip on a layer of **Jägermeister** and finally dribble **cranberry juice** on top. The juice will probably slide down to create a marbled effect. That should get your head swimming.

Patti's Passion

We've **no idea** who Patti was, but she **certainly** left an **impression** on one shooter-maker.

Her drink consists of a layer of **Kahlua** and a second one of **Irish cream.**

For the full effect, it must be gulped down **without** using your **hands.**

Just cover the glass with your mouth, tip back your head and **swallow.**

Pecker Wrecker

This is strictly a drink for **boys'** night out, so don't blame us if you get home to a less than enthusiastic reception from Mamma **afterwards.** Traditionally you make a whole cocktail shaker of it and just **pour** the shooters all evening, knocking them back happily as long as they (or you) **last.**

Mix equal quantities of **cranberry** juice, **pineapple** juice, **Crème de Noyaux,** or any nut-flavoured liqueur, and **blackberry brandy.** Shake over **ice** and pour into shot glasses. Very more-ish indeed.

Pousse Café

This is the **bright** French drink that can probably claim to be the **first** shooter invented.
It was created to **add colour** at the end of a good meal, and depended as much on looks as **flavour** for its **appeal**.
It was probably introduced to the New World by a Canadian barman of French ancestry.

Use any number of **contrasting** colours, layering each carefully on top of the previous one.
A typical recipe might be red **grenadine** at the bottom, then clear **Cointreau,** followed by green **crème de menthe,** golden **Galliano,** and finally a dark **brandy.**
That's a real test of your pouring skill!

Ruby Red

An attractive little **pick-me-up**, that can be merged, or made to look **very pretty** with **careful** layering.

Start with a layer of **cranberry juice,** float a generous layer of **vodka** on top and finish with a few drops of fresh **lemon juice** to add a sting.

Russian Candy

This little drink gets its
Russian name from the vodka.
The rest is **pure sweetness.**

Start with the **vodka**, slide a layer
of **peach schnapps** on top and finally
dribble a little **grenadine** syrup over the top.
The red syrup will slide down the sides of the glass
to give an attractive swirling effect.

Satan's Mouthwash

They say this **evil** little drink will **cure** you of pure thoughts if you hold it in your **mouth** for a while **before** swallowing it.

Start with a layer of **black sambuca,** and top it with an equal layer of **Jack Daniel's.** You can also swirl them together for a dramatic effect.

Sex on the Beach

There are many different versions of this drink, but they are all **colourful**, look *inviting* and taste **divine**. The layered versions also require a steady hand.

Mix **Midori** melon liqueur, **grenadine**, **pineapple** juice and **cranberry** juice. Pour into a glass and top with a layer of **vodka**.

You can also experiment with layering these ingredients. It might take some time to find the correct order, depending on the specific gravities.

Silk Panties

This is an **attractive**, and quite **sophisticated**, little drink. Some say it derived its name from the **smooth** way it **slips down**, which was probably a serious case of late-night wishful thinking.

Start with a layer of **black sambuca** and carefully slide a layer of clear **peach schnapps** on top. **Looks** good, tastes **good**.

Slippery Nipple

Nobody could resist a drink with a name like **this**, particularly if an **attractive** barmaid sidles up and offers you one. Well, a man can **dream**, can't he?

Half-fill a shot glass with
black sambuca and carefully
pour a layer of **Irish cream** on top,
taking care not to mix the two.
Slide the drink down in a slow, nonstop gulp.

Splash
of Passion

This shooter is said by some to derive its name from its **looks** and **colour**. Those who claim to know about these things, say it's really named for its **taste**. We'll leave it up to you to decide. It's easy to make but, to get the best out of it, there's a technique to **downing** it properly!

Start with a layer of **lime cordial** and top it with an equal layer of **Irish cream**. **Take it** all into your mouth and **hold it** for as long as you can before **swallowing**.

Slips down all warm and suggestive, hey!

Squashed Frog

In spite of the **gross name** (and you don't need much imagination to realize how it was named), this is a **sweet** and **tangy** drink.

Start with a deepish layer of
Advokaat liqueur, slip on a
smaller layer of **crème de menthe** and
trickle a swirl of red **grenadine** over the top.
It looks **gruesome** enough to make
anybody croak!

Suitcase

Pack your mouth around this one,
but don't get too carried away.

Fill one shot glass with **Jack Daniel's**
and another with **passionfruit** cordial.
Swish the passionfruit cordial around in your
mouth for as long as you can, then
add the Jack Daniel's without swallowing.
Swish some more, then **swallow.**

You could **substitute** the passionfruit
with **lime** cordial and call it a Briefcase.

Hot Mexican

Perhaps it's because there's so much **hard work** and **ceremony** attached to this drink that it got its **rather** odd name.

You'll need half a glass of **beer** to start, and have a slice of **fresh lime** standing by.
In a shot glass, mix equal parts of **tequila** and **white rum.** Light the top and drop it quickly into the beer glass.
Drink it down, **down,** down.
Then follow with the slice of lime. **Olé**!

Tequila Smash

Here's a **lively** number to get the party off to a **bubbly** start.

Place a layer of **tequila** at the bottom of the shot glass and top carefully with **7-Up** or any clear fizzy drink. Place a hand over the top and **slam** it onto the bar counter to get the shooter **fizzing**. **Swallow** it in a single gulp, gas and all.
If you burp within 10 seconds, you have to take another one.
For a colourful variation, try **raspberry** soda.

Twister

Here's a **nice** little shooter to try your *layering* skills.

Start with a layer of **Southern Comfort,**
slip a layer of **tequila** on top of that and
end with a layer of **vodka.**
Let it slip down slowly so you get the flavours
in three separate parts.

Undertaker

This triple-decker is not as **grim** as its name might suggest. The most it will do is take you **under the table.**

Start with a layer of **Cointreau,** add a layer of **Jägermeister** and finish off with a layer of **white rum.**

Lower away.

Woo-woo Shooter

This is an **easy** little shooter for the
steady-handed, and is always a **popular** choice.

Pour a dollop of **cranberry juice** into
a shot glass and float on a layer of
peach schnapps.
Top up carefully with **vodka.**
The name is probably derived from the cries of
approval of the drinker.

747

You may even **take off** after **fuelling** up on a **few** of these.

Start with a layer of **Kahlua**,
slide on a layer of **Amaretto** and top with
a layer of **Irish cream.**

No more economy, from now on you'll be flying
First Class all the way.

Index

Picture credits

All photographs by **Danie Nel Photography** for New Holland Image
Library, ©NHIL, with the exception of the following:
Struik Image Library/Ryno: Cover; p16 (right);
21 (below left & right); 22; 158
Stockbyte: p8; 32
galloimages/gettyimages.com: p11.

Acknowledgements

The author and publisher would like to thank
the **Bartender's Workshop** and **Industry**, Cape Town,
for providing staff and premises for the photoshoot.
Thanks also to Christelle Marais and Danie Nel
for styling and props.

Those who enjoy alcohol, do so responsibly.